Looking In, Looking Out

Best wishes,
Shanta Acharya
30 May 2008

Also by Shanta Acharya

Poetry
Numbering Our Days' Illusions (Rockingham Press, UK; 1995)
Not This, Not That (Rupa & Co, India; 1994)

Studies in American Literature
The Influence of Indian Thought on Ralph Waldo Emerson (The Edwin Mellen Press, USA; 2001)

Business
Asset Management: Equities Demystified (John Wiley & Sons, UK; 2002)
Investing In India (Macmillan, UK; 1998)

For more information visit: www.shantaacharya.com

Looking In, Looking Out

Shanta Acharya

HEADLAND

First published in 2005
by
HEADLAND PUBLICATIONS
38 York Avenue
West Kirby, Wirral
CH48 3JF

Copyright © 2005 Shanta Acharya

British Library Cataloguing in Publication Data.
A full CIP record for this book is available from the British Library
ISBN
1 902096 89 4

All rights reserved. No part of this publication may be reproduced, stored in a retrieval system, or transmitted in any form, or by any means, electronic, mechanical, photocopying, recording or otherwise, without the prior written permission of the publisher.

Requests to publish work from this book must be sent to Headland Publications.

Shanta Acharya has asserted her right under Section 77 of the Copyright, Designs and Patents Act 1988 to be identified as the author of this book.

Printed in Great Britain by
L. Cocker Ltd.
Unit A9, Prospect Street, Liverpool L6 1AU

HEADLAND acknowledges the financial
assistance of Arts Council England

CONTENTS

At The Edge Of The World	9
The Annunciation	10
The Saviour	11
The Vision Of St John	12
Making Faces	13
The Milkmaid	14
Lost In Africa	15
Xochipilli	16
Yashoda's Vision	17
The Art Of Eating Fruits	18
Of Magic And Men	19
Perhaps	20
Bharata Natyam	21
The Three Graces	22
Some People	23
Special	24
What Is There To Know?	25
What You Don't Know	26
Snowdrops	27
Survival	28
Ichthys	29
Our First Meeting	30
Living Without Cleopatra	31
The Fly And The Bee	32
Of Poems	33
The Scriptwriter	35
To Be A Beginner	36
A Poet's RSVP	37
Poetry Reading	38

CONTENTS *continued*

Job Hunting	39
The Singing Bird	41
The Kiss	42
Prescription For Glasses	43
Experience And Innocence	44
Daily Remedies	45
Bachelors Soup	46
Azaleas In Spring	47
Flight Distance	48
Mrs Kafka's Dilemma	49
Broken Glass	51
Taking Stock	52
Celebration	53
Fickle Flame	54
Mirrors	55
Sleeping Beauty	56
Patience	57
Earthing Live Wires	58
Dear Tech Support	59
Dear Customer	60
The Hour Glass	61
My Good Luck Home	62
Looking In, Looking Out	63

Acknowledgements

I would like to thank the editors of the following publications in which several of these poems appeared, sometimes in earlier versions:

Acumen, Aesthetica: A Review of Contemporary Artists, Agenda, Ambit, A Glass Of New Made Wine (Poetry Salzburg), *Coffee House Poetry, Confluence, Connections: The Literary Scene In The South, Critical Survey, Envoi, Exile, Fire, In The Company Of Poets* (Hearing Eye), *Home* (Katabasis), *Iota Poetry Quarterly, Masala* (Macmillan Children's Books), *Moving Worlds, Mslexia, New Hope International, ORBIS Quarterly International Literary Journal, Oxford Quarterly Review, Planet – The Welsh Internationalist, Plant Care: A Festschrift for Mimi Khalvati* (Linda Lee Books), *Poetry London Newsletter, Poetry Street, Poetry Today, Pulsar, Seam, Spokes Poetry Magazine, The Bound Spiral, The Frogmore Papers, The Interpreter's House, The Redbeck Anthology of British South Asian Poetry, The Swansea Review, Velocity: the Best of Apples & Snakes, Wasafiri* and *World Literature Written In English* in the **UK**.

Six Seasons Review in **Bangladesh**, *The Toronto Review* in **Canada**, *Paris/ Atlantic* in **France**, *Chandrabhaga, India International Centre Quarterly, Indian Literature, Journal of Literature and Aesthetics, The Indian P.E.N., Poets International, Poetry Chain, The Journal of the Poetry Society, Kavya Bharati* and *Samyukta: A Journal of Women's Studies* in **India**, *Poetry New Zealand* in **New Zealand**, *Cimarron Review, Mother Earth International* and *South Asian Review* in the **USA**.

I am also grateful to editors of websites where several of these poems appear.

For
Sanjay and *Binodini*
Sushanta and *Madhumita*
Bikash and always for *Bapa* and *Ma*

Just Infinites of Nought –
As far as it could see –
So looked the face I looked upon –
So looked itself – on Me –
Emily Dickinson

What is life but the angle of vision? A man is measured by the angle at which he looks at objects. . . . This is his fate and his employer. Knowing is the measure of man.
Ralph Waldo Emerson

At The Edge Of The World
(After Anish Kapoor's *'creations'* at the Hayward Gallery, 1998)

The queue outside stretches
like an alley cat, waiting
to enter the crowded gallery,
explore the plugged-holes at the centre
of walls and ceilings. Not enough time,
space for all to experience ways of defining
It; of lending shape, colour, sound, meaning.

Once inside, the world is turned upside down,
inside out, disoriented through double mirrors,
emptied of space funnelling into *arupa*,
untitled, leaving us newly-born, fearful of oblivion.

In the beginning (or is it the end?)
securing a discrete position
I get sucked into my mother's womb
peering at deep dark shrines of
my body, her body; our bodies
moving in rhythm to creations
at the vortex, doubly-inverted images,
when I become pregnant, making the world many.

We exchange according to our measure
the open-endedness of things; configuring
a nose, a breast, a man posing in his briefs?
Or something new waiting to be seen.

Imagination turns earth and stone into sky.
In the dark, polished hollow of a marble mummy,
a fleeting spirit appears. A twisting column of light,
I flicker before giving up the ghost.

The Annunciation

The book she held half-open, half-closed,
clasped between startled fingers,
her thumb, a page mark; the others curled
gently over the covers, slightly ajar.

Seized in a moment of contemplation, the spirit
of quiet ravishment had not quite effaced her.

The rich maroon and purple-blue sleeves of her dress,
embroidered with golden borders, caress the letters
of the illuminated script as the light of Gabriel
intercepted the direction of her thoughts.

The painting was a silent church
before the service begins. A time for waiting.
Did Mary have a premonition of portentous tidings;
did she comprehend the divine dispensation?

What were her thoughts when that voice was heard,
her trance shattered with the dove's laser beams?
What was the book she clasped in her hands,
her memoirs or a book of prayers?

What was Mary doing dressed like a queen
seated among the lilies and roses,
as if waiting for a rendezvous with a secret lover ?
Did she feel the stirrings in her womb,
great white wings flapping?

The Saviour
(After the icon by *Andrey Rublyov*)

The passion in your eyes penetrates
every nook and cranny of me, illuminating
deep down things leaving me
rejuvenated like the arrival of spring.

I try hard to take in the guide's lecture –
"Very little is known of his life;
chronicles say he was a monk.
Frescoes in the Annunciation Cathedral
of the Kremlin were painted by
him, Andrey Rublyov, and Theophanes.
Rublyov also created the icons in the Dormition Cathedral
in Vladimir in 1408. His *Trinity*,
the greatest masterpiece of Russian art,
was created for the Trinity-St Sergius Monastery.
The paintings were destroyed in the 17th century ..."
Her voice fades as the tourist group
dissolves in the Tretyakov gallery.

High there, unable to shake off your stare
resuscitating me with lungfuls of air,
I return to majesty's gashed gold-vermilion,
worship at the frayed edges of perfection.

The Vision Of St John
(After El Greco's *The Opening of the Fifth Seal* *)

Bodies elongated, perspective distorted,
colours incandescent, transfigured –

I saw underneath the alter the souls of them
that had been slain for the word of God ...

And there was given to each one of them a
white robe; and it was said unto them
they should rest yet for a little season...

Martyred souls like naked bathers cover
each other in sheets of white, green and amber.

Kneeling he stands, hands outstretched
touching the void, clad in a robe of sapphire.

For those in agony there may be hope –
we arrive here sick and broken
to mend in this life, this earth our hospital.

The light in the altarpiece is apocalyptic;
figures dematerialised, quickened by grace
demanding communion.

* El Greco's unfinished painting was for the Tavera Hospital in
Toledo, Spain.

Making Faces
(After George Grosz' *Fruhlingsanfang*)

Her fragile features float
above the voices
rising, falling, swirling,
grand ballerinas of smoke
pirouetting on cigars, pipes
balanced between fat lips
of aging men, moustached,
dark-suited and solid
on coffee tables encircling her.

The painting caricatures
all the characters in it,
depicting the times' depravity;
except this porcelain, unreal face
in *The Beginning of Spring*,
threatening to melt under closer
scrutiny, yet haunting the picture.

Her older, frisky escort knows well
the irresistible rising of sap in life's autumn,
a crescendo of notes in symphony;
a darkening sky illuminated with fireworks,
upwardly mobile sperms shooting
forth like champion sprinters, overcoming
odds, with a fascination for making faces,
creating a world of cartoon characters.

The Milkmaid
(After the painting by *Johannes Vermeer*)

Concentrating on the milk she pours
from one earthenware vessel to another;

The mustard yellow sleeves of her
rolled-up blouse revealing her sturdy arms;

The beige, purple and maroon
of her garment in flowing folds swoon –

Highlighting her sumptuous, robust figure.
The light catches her in a moment of stillness,

Head bent slightly as if in prayer.
Brightness of freshly baked bread

Spread invitingly on the table in front of her,
the kitchen utensils, a basket of wicker;

The foot-warmer resting on the floor
in one corner offer hints and guesses – nurture

With passion, a sensual aspect to her character.
Her attention is not lavished on the viewer.

Lost In Africa
(After the Royal Academy Of Arts' *Africa: The Art of a Continent* exhibition)

Look, the hand axe from Olduvai
over a million and half years ago
among the first things made by man,
no earlier artefact exists in museums –

Much later the arrival of the decorated
ostrich egg, needing no messenger
hot foot from the Nile to tell a bushman
that an egg is a ready-made pot.

The five thousand year old battlefield palette
(its two pieces brought together for the first time),
depicts a disfigured continent
the scars, the wars; the idyllic scenes of man and beast –
the Jekyll and Hyde union perfectly captured
in the Makonde helmet mask.

The showcase of the sensuous lips of Akhenaten,
the seductive torso of Nefertiti,
the haunting head of their daughter reveal
only the artist's attention to detail;
no directions here to the status of women.

Woodcarvings from the Eastern coast
enriched by trade, smeared with toil
display the skill in carving objects
from a single piece of wood. Exquisite
the diadems of lions, crocodiles, snakes,
an ivory profile of a leopard's head –
dreaming of ancestral homes lost in Africa.

Xochipilli

Your journey from the island of herons
past the crooked mountains
to the place of the stone cactus
where an eagle perched on a prickly pear
and the first Templo Mayor was born
took centuries; longer
to create a civilisation carved in stone
painted in blood, consecrated by gods

Who sacrificed themselves to make
the sun, moon, mankind and maize.
To sustain the cycle of creation, the Aztecs fed
the gods with human hearts and blood.
Divinity was all! Flower Prince –

God of poetry and plants, patron of song and dance,
you presided over public ceremonies,
staged battles with ritually dressed warriors
capturing the enemy for sacrifice.
The priests clad in robes of gods,
transformed with juice of the cactus.

Posing for us at the Royal Academy of Arts
Xochipilli, do you feel at home –
seated upright, cross-legged on a decorated
seat, each side depicting a flower
with a butterfly sucking its nectar,
your limbs tattooed with flowers,
magnificent your mask with hollowed-eyes,
chipped nose, lips parted in a wry smile;
your head-dress ornate with large ear spools
as much in vogue as your necklace
from the skin of the head of a jaguar?

Yashoda's Vision

Krishna, barely past crawling on all fours,
full of a child's curiosity and love,
eager to devour the world –

Is one day accused of eating dirt.
His playmates complain to Yashoda,
Krishna's foster mother
who unable to ignore matters further
is forced to chide her charge; she commands
Krishna to reveal the contents of his mouth.

As she kneels to peer inside this cavern,
she witnesses the birth of the universe –
the sun, moon, stars, galaxies,
the oceans, earth, deserts, volcanoes,
animals and plants long extinct,
time, love, death, birth, pain, wisdom, ecstasy;
not a life, leaf, stone, word, person missing.

Yashoda sees herself, all her past
incarnations, with all the dirt, the dust
of the universe in its place; for a moment
blessed with insight, the essence of Creation…

The Art Of Eating Fruits

Dig a hole in the eye of the green coconut,
turn it upside down and drink all the milk it has to offer;
split it open, scrape the kernel, deep inside its belly,
then let the tender flesh slide down your gullet.

Hold the mango in the palm of your hands,
firmly seize the day with the gentleness of passion
as you close your eyes, squeezing and sucking a breast.
Sitting in the garden without knives, forks or spoons; knead
the yielding flesh, lick the sweetness oozing from the fruit.

Crack open the pomegranate like a brittle skull;
rubies lie hidden there, waiting to be crushed by diamonds
sparkling in your mouth. If you prefer *anar* juice, grind
the jewels into a vermilion paste as if preparing for *holi* –
smear the colours on friends, turn them into modern paintings
instead of a canvass with finely chiselled, miniature portraits.

Pull back the skin of a banana with nonchalance,
bite off greedily its erectness; afraid it might
oxidise into a limpid, rusty brown. Have no patience.

Unseeded dates are most pleasurable crunching
through their crepe fibres; seedless grapes, plums, prunes
are best munched with the skin to imbibe their full flavour.

The art of eating jackfruit is acquired only by the *artiste*.
Protect hands with surgically oiled gloves of knowledge
before you prise it open, diving into its ambergris.

Of Magic And Men

In a Hindu world of fantasy and fable,
myths, legends, gods and demons,
irrationality appears reasonable –

The clear light of day obfuscates while chaos enlightens.

Liberals argue: "If our gods can eat and sleep,
steal buttermilk, make love, fall ill,
go visit their aunt in full regalia,
even brushing their teeth before partying,
what's so surprising about drinking some milk?
After all, it has been one long, hot, desiccating summer!"

The believers devoutly rejoice: "To us, a saviour is born!"
As long as a search does not a multitude of child-gods spawn.

When a community unites in a willing suspension of disbelief,
experts agree it is acknowledging a deeper human need
to rise above the insignificance of our existence,
embrace the Beyond that represents our notions of God.
The world's a stage, remember? So, question not the need.

Ganesha and Nandi, Lord Shiva's bull, suck milk
simultaneously in various temples in the world.
TV cameras religiously broadcast these scenes
from a multitude of angles that prove or disprove nothing.

"It is all in the mind:" the guru-busters explain.
Their patience like the roots of a banyan tree
reaches out to educate the superstitious earth.

Magicians are no god-men; the making of ashes,
trinkets and rings do not amount to miracles.

Even tough Seshan's degree in physics does not free him.
Sai Baba bends his mind with a *navratna* ring;
out goes his hard-headed, Harvard training!

Both sides remain united in the struggle.
God's in heaven and all's wrong with our world –
except miracles unfurl daily to the faithful
not impervious to the mystery of the universe.

Perhaps
(For *Nissim Ezekiel*)

Perhaps we were never meant
to be like other creatures
more at home in their environment;
driven by instincts, their natures.

We pine for what we are not
and cannot be, for the moment
we are what we wanted to be, we want
to move on; our desires already spent.

Perhaps, being unhappy, never feeling at home
is our only hope, our promised salvation;
who can tell where this need will take us
as we pursue self-discovery to our satisfaction?

Bharata Natyam

The dancer's inaugural prayer
establishes the connection between all beings:
her *Kauthuvam* to Ganesha, Kali and Nataraja
transforms London's Bloomsbury Theatre
into the precincts of a temple panoplied with stories.

We are transported into the arena of gods and goddesses.
Dancer, devotees, replica of sculptures
on Tanjore temples, come alive with chanting of *slokas*.

This *devadasi* explains the intricacies of classical
Indian dance to an audience uncertain of itself –
its notions of Truth, God and Love.

Her *Varnam*, eternal search of the lover
for the beloved concealed in *maya*,
smoke gets in your eyes when there is fire in your heart.

Bharata: *bhav*a, *ra*ga, *ta*la; expression, melody, rhythm.
Her inner state of being mirrored in *abhinaya*.
Musical notes of *raga charukesi* embellish the mood
adorning her *ghunghroos' adi-tala* beat.

When hands can speak, eyes can kill, feet can draw –
bodies move in spheres of mystic law.

The white garland of jasmine on her swinging plait
is a snake enchanted by the charmer's twisted reed.

While the dance is on a spell is on us all;
dancer and dance, we remain enthralled.

The Three Graces

They sit on Time's trireme,
triplets posing for their triptych.
Enthroned in the centre is Present,
Janus-faced, phoenix-like perishes; is reborn,
cannot reconcile her schizophrenic selves.
This female Gemini caught between
Future and Past, jealously guards the
umbilical corridor connecting women.

Looking through an illusion, arrangement
of mirrors creating life-images
in the prism-womb of time and space,
wearing spectacles to correct human eyes –
the mind recollecting the past,
though not in tranquillity; dreaming
of a future sealed from human beings.
The third eye is a gift for Present,
the 360-degree angle of vision.

Future is the fairest of all – beckoning
us to new horizons, promising heaven…
Past is enchanting too, transforming herself
in the chameleon looking-glass of Time
turning everything outside in, downside up
as self-preservation takes over, shaking
each other like pieces in a kaleidoscope,
refracting memories through magical glasses;
three witches flying, casting spells…

There is no way out –
they hypnotise each other and the onlookers.

Some People
(For *Ava*)

Some people are better avoided.
Some people seem unable to survive
except on the brink of self-inflicted disaster.
Chaos is the elixir of their life,
chaos that never leads to order.

Some people dream of changing the world
aided by religion, power or lack of self worth;
hurricane-like destroying all that crosses their path.
They are never seen after the devastation
to do the honourable thing;
    accept blame, make amends.

.Some people are never willing to make a mistake.
They go a long way out of their way
to maintain the status quo.
Never able to take a risk, anything new is rejected
with suspicion; often passing for tradition and heritage.
Their tunnel vision leads not to joy or enlightenment.

Some people fail to see life straight and simple.
They misinterpret things with such passion,
such formidable knowledge and eloquence;
their sound and fury signifying nothing.

Get to know them, if you must, with an open mind –
only forgive them their limitations and trespasses
as we must learn to forgive ourselves.

Special

There is so much good in the worst of us,
And so much bad in the best of us,
That is hardly becomes any of us
To talk about the rest of us.
     Anonymous

There is nothing special about you or me
except our thinking that makes it so.
Some grow up thinking they are special,
others do so imagining they are not so.
It is our parents' caring or the lack of it
that makes us feel special or not quite so;
not the way we were made by our Maker.
That recognition comes in life much later.

Most nations believe they are special.
People who've lived together as neighbours,
suddenly turn against each other and fight for years.
Others declare war for no special reason or purpose.

Most races think they are superior to others.
each race has its Hitler and its Jews.
We are all so special that in time we all must disappear.
In the interim, we pay the price for being *special*
not knowing it was worth paying for.

There are times for feeling special,
times for remembering and doing things special,
knowing always it is our participation that makes it so.

There is nothing special about you or me,
there is much that is special about each one of us –
it is our thinking that makes it thus.

What Is There To Know?

That a quarter of the world's people live in poverty
without adequate access to food, shelter, education or health.
That the natural resources of our world are limited.
That in less than twenty years' time there will be millions of
Chinese men wanting to marry foreign women.
That what happens in the Middle East or Africa concerns us.
That in the next decade in Japan and in Europe
old people will die suddenly of strange illnesses,
but the younger family members will not complain.
That the need to develop trade will unite Europe.
That there will be no real distinction between
the major political parties in most nations.
That all over the world politicians will be marginalized,
the state will wither away and Marx will have the last laugh.
That more and more people will work less and less;
and some people will never have any work experience.
That technology, finance and leisure will boom.
That more and more men and women will remain single
but have families with different lovers and friends.
That injustice will live as long as human beings do,
but hope, love and truth have a way of surviving too.
That damaged people are not always dangerous.
That while honey, garlic, ginger are good for you
charity, laughter, sleep and exercise are better.
That snakes are as noble as other creatures on earth
and will not bite unless provoked and most are non-poisonous.
That most murderers know their victims.
That every day is a miracle despite what we don't do.
That children give us a chance to change our world.
That each one of us is a very special person,
That each one of us needs to discover this truth.

What You Don't Know

As a child you instinctively know
there are things you don't know;
you also know you know of things
the adults think you don't know.

Growing up is a process of knowing,
of knowing that you don't know;
acknowledging others might know,
though they don't know that you don't know.

Wisdom comes when you can forget what you know,
when you know parents, friends, lovers, well-wishers,
even your enemies, your best teachers, don't know;
for what is worth knowing is what you don't know.

Some people are born plain lucky;
they sail through life without knowing
that they don't know, and not knowing
they don't know what is worth knowing
protects them from a lifetime of unknowing.

For most of us there is a price to be paid,
most of us get damaged, more or less, in the process
and end up knowing what is not worth knowing.

Snowdrops

In the shadow of tall, sky-gazing trees
a convent of reclusive snowdrops
face the earth, bent in meditation.

Possessed in the white heat of passion,
the gravity of their thoughts weigh them down,
their porcelain faces averted from our direction.

In translucent stems of jade and petals of pearls
they arrive bearing the gift of life; nuns of peace,
breaking out of barren winter's embrace.

Messengers of hope, figurines of faith and charity,
fragile creations oozing dignity –
they give according to their measure,
demanding nothing in return; their miniature
stature, lacking fragrance not colour.

They bow, emptying themselves of all desire,
make peace with themselves, without walking on fire.

Survival

At the summer solstice, the sun
in Cancer breeds vulnerable,
tenacious, excitable
crustaceans programmed to triumph
against odds; in water, on land,
balancing their destiny
with grace, not unlike women
in the developing world
transporting water, stones, children,
with their dignity, grace
on their heads, shoulders, arms –
the body transformed into
a miracle, a vessel for survival.

Crabs, lobsters, beetles, scarabs,
snails, turtles, tortoises –
all self-contained, sensitive creatures –
carry their crosses on their backs
negotiating in an uncertain,
unpredictable, unforgiving world;
making themselves at home everywhere,
being eternally prepared.

Alert to their surroundings,
shielding themselves from danger,
they adorn their armour –
faith that arrives like leaves in spring.
For these guiltless warriors,
only one out of a hundred
of thousands will survive their spawning.

Ichthys

That we were here first has been universally recognised
except by some monsters on terra firma who behave as if
they own this world; they make fun of us, call us names,
represent us riding bicycles or shove us up their smelly spouts
and nostrils, not the sort of places we normally like to visit.
Not that we lack a sense of humour; but enough is enough.

It was mainly the fault of that god-man who used us for his
miracles. Since then we have been a symbol of him.
Some species are backward in their understanding.
Why he could not settle for fruits or some other plant
is beyond us. We like to help, we are generous;
we feed all manner of creatures with our flesh
but prefer not to call it a miracle or holy communion.
We never imagined it would become a global phenomenon.

We would like to wipe out hunger in Africa, keep the world
healthy with our contribution to research in medicine
but we do not like wars that are fought on our territory
by those who have nothing in common with us. Our homes
are uninhabitable; we are left to survive anyway we can,
our gills stuck with oil, unable to breathe. Luckily, we know
how to multiply but humans have yet to learn how to divide.

We do not like to be a commodity subject to demand and supply,
even the most imaginative ones refer to us as sex symbols.
We have entered a language that constricts our purpose and meaning
appearing without copyright on seals, rings, urns and tombstones.

Our First Meeting
(For *Ashish, Arup* and *Aditi*)

My neighbour, who lives alone in the attic, comes
home at awkward hours, and suddenly leaves;
disturbing me in my random patterns of sleep, as he goes
about his business, when the world restores itself in peace.

It is difficult to say if he has a nine to five job,
it appears he's a bit of a loner and does not hobnob.
He scurries around clumsily like an Underground rat in a hurry.
I used to think of him rudely as a fat pigeon worth a curry.

The walls of my ceiling are thin and my ears rather sharp,
I found his walkabouts unpredictable but settled not to carp.
Having resolved to ferret out his mysterious ways;
Get to know the enemy I chanted, sleeping soundly most days.

One wintry afternoon, I heard him dancing on the rafters
having swung in from the branches of the neighbouring trees.
Whether he was drunk, merry or suicidal, was not easy to tell.
I was making some *masala* tea to pick me up; I felt like hell.

With murder on my mind, time appeared ripe for us to meet.
I opened the entrance to my attic, careful not
to frighten my rent-evading, tax-dodging tenant.
He was prepared too; never beat a retreat.

It was dark as twilight can be. I switched on the light
to see two shining ruby eyes staring back at me.
We stared and stared as it was love at first sight,
my big, brown, bushy squirrel of a neighbour and me.

The question mark on his tail unfurled in a farewell and greeting;
we turned away together never to forget our first meeting.

Living Without Cleopatra
(For *Jaysinh Birjépatil*)

From her lair Cleopatra saw the bronze full moon
hanging like Captain Ahab's doubloon,
high on the mast of heaven,
reward for sighting the forsworn Other, the enemy within.

The moon was almost exactly at dead noon
in the sky-clock of the window when she woke in pain.
At the end of her memory there was dampness,
years of darkness as she struggled to remember.

The scene in the distance was an advent calendar
with some windows lighted with goodwill messages.
The clock inside Cleopatra was ticking too fast.
Cleopatra dreamed and sighed for her Antony.

He had been a sprightly puppy before disease and age
lathered him with fat. He breathed his last with his shiny
nose seeking her paws; their communication encompassing
the vastness of time and space as age withered her
and poor demented Cleopatra went barking mad,
baying at the moon as if she saw her Antony there.

One moonstruck night, Cleopatra sighted the forsworn enemy
and lunged at the double moon swimming in the pool.
Breathless, out of practice, she drowned to join her Antony;
her whole world buried in the moving, waning moon.

The Fly And The Bee

'I am equally at ease
with the sacred or the profane.
I can sit indifferently
on sacramental offerings
or on things most foul to beings,
at home in both,
bearing the good with the evil,
hankering for neither.
I have that rare option.'
The fly boasted to the bee
with some exaggeration.

'I can only sit on blossoms
ready for pollination,
sucking the nectar of flowers
or in my honeycomb
dreaming of perfumed stalks.'
Lamented the bee acknowledging
its limitations with graceful candour.

Of Poems

I

They seldom arrive at your door ringing your bell
like the postman with a registered letter or parcel,
friends for dinner, Friends of the Earth,
or even the truant monsters from hell.

They are more inclined to trespass your thoughts,
your dreams, appearing with their gifts
unannounced, unexpected –
flying in and out, colourful birds of passage
demanding your undivided attention,
regardless of your present situation
whether you are falling asleep, shopping,
engaged in a business meeting.

They expect you to drop everything,
be eternally ready for their reception.
Some arrive perfectly composed, poised
babies with perfect teeth and backbone,
demanding to be heard, seeking adoration;
some need to be rescued urgently
with extensive surgery before they start breathing;
others are lost irretrievably; staying on
in memory to haunt your lack of skill in delivery.

II

Poems are no different than children –
at first clinging to your inner being and soul,
inhabiting your body's every cell,
a permanent physical condition, oxygen in your blood;
defining your sanity, your personality,
any life you might claim to be your own.

Before you know they're born, they are rehearsing
eagerly to fly away, explore their place in the world.

Inexperienced and naive, they are often easily led,
the weakest ones the most susceptible,
trusting strangers with a honeyed tongue,
ready to strike up a dialogue, pretend being grown-up.
Like many adults, they end up lonely and misunderstood.

If one achieves any sort of distinction, the others
temporarily bask in the refracted glory of success.
If one is dishonoured, the rest are condemned to oblivion
though the family stands solidly behind,
providing undying support, proof of pedigree.

Years later, having seen the world, survived its slings,
embraced its wicked ways, returns the prodigal son.

With a shock of recognition you observe a child honing home
with the curve of your lip, the bend in your eyebrow;
and you remember fondly the time of its making,
when the word was made flesh, conceived and born.

The Scriptwriter

You demanded alterations everyday,
you, whom I invented for a very special purpose.
I yielded to your preferences, noted the things you loved.

You wanted your separate exits and entrances,
yearned for a life that I would curse no one with.
I indulged your fantasies, imagining you would tire of it all

Sooner or later, leaving your world to me.
Your characters asked to be born and I let it be so.
But the text had to be changed to suit your silly plans,
the plot went crazy and my story floundered.

After all these mistakes, you'd think humility is possible;
as the scriptwriter I can urge you to be sensible?

I asked you to be yourselves when I delivered you,
freeing you to overcome sadness and temptation.
How can I write when you restrict my meaning?

To Be A Beginner

If the angel deigns to come, it will be because you have convinced him, not with tears, but with your humble resolve to be always beginning: to be a beginner!
Rainer Maria Rilke

The master artist triumphant,
celebrated by critics, feted by fans,
confessed to his favourite disciple
the secret of Art, the compulsion to create
endless versions of the same
as each one came out irrevocably flawed.

The idea of perfection pervaded his dreams
even after a different world was revealed to him.

Each day arrived wearing its diadem of gifts.
Carpe diem, carpe diem, carpe diem –
he trilled like a thrush from the highest branch in spring,
never fully understanding its meaning.

He had yet to learn a few things, including
the art of removing the mote in his eye.

Never near enough divinity, he could not
see the connection between beings.

In his solitariness he could not experience
the mysteries of the universe nor be enlightened
with its promise of beginnings,
trusting the light would descend on him
the day angels sing.

A Poet's RSVP

I am preoccupied, I have been thinking –
sorry I cannot come to your dinner-party;
like judge and jury I must keep my own company.

I need the time and space for myself
to wander in the courtyard of the moonstruck sky,
to contemplate the genesis of our religions,
the unwritten history of our nations, to comprehend
the state of our present human institutions
for only then can I move on to universes beyond.

I have this vocation; I have to live, pray and wait
for life's meaning to unfold itself to me.

I am unable to sleep watching the changing
of the sky at night, God's pied beauty, knowing
that several wars still rage around me,
that not enough is being done to eliminate
the world's hunger, sickness and injustice.

I have no answers, only a head full of questions.
I need to exercise and meditate, train myself
to unravel life's dappled quality, its virtual reality.

I need to shop, cook, clean, I need aeons to dream.
I have unquenchable desires that will not be slaked
with your rich party food, dance, drink, drugs or men.

Let me be, dear friend, on my own but do keep in touch.
Thank you for asking; very sorry I cannot come.

Poetry Reading

How much pep talk does a poem need?
If the poem speaks not for itself,
alas, the poet must speak!

We exchange our books to explore
the subtle enclosures of our mind –
a poem, a stanza, a line, a phrase
that deserves a space in living memory.

Sometimes, out of the blue, a stranger
buys a book and wants it autographed.

Many of these poems are decades old –
brewing in me, barrels of fine wine, unsold!
Forget what you know, let it's meaning unfold.

Enroute to the pub, tramps come and go,
the talk at the pub is mumbo-jumbo.

The night is jet-lagged. I sleepwalk
to the Underground station, hurtling across
cyberspace and global market forces.

Job Hunting

My application
supplication
duplication
transfiguration
for a position

In their company
was graced by
an interview
in a room without a view
with the chairman
and board members few.

While words flowed
coffee stirred, eyes waltzed
questions lay dangerously forked
on painted china, double entendre.

After the initial screening
I was ushered in
for an aptitude test in
the boss's limousine.

As he breathed all over me
a Maharaja's grin spiced with whisky
fangs bared, moustache caressing
cheek bones, with double-fat lining –
he promised me a job in
exchange of favours titillating.

The prospect of which
gave me gooseflesh
and I was a porcupine
driving through The Serpentine.

Saying I would consider
his extraordinary offer,
I flew out of his car
landing in Leicester Square.

Accosted by a tramp, later
for a few pennies from heaven
I explode: "F—k off, you lecher!"

For which I was sorry
as I heard him stutter –
"What is the matter?
No need to be rude dear,
just wanted change for a cuppa…"

I silently handed him a fiver
saying nothing further.

"God bless ya…"
I heard him singing after
me as I was lost
in the twilight rush hour.

The Singing Bird

The day he disappeared with a note signed
In memory of the good times we've had
glued to the gilded cage with the singing bird,
she took stock of her situation
and came to the conclusion –
an unexamined life is not worth living...

That evening, in the process of easing
the dead weight in her life
with the *Pathétique* and several glasses of gin,
she made a short list of things
to be done in no particular order:

- Get a complete make over – face, clothes, shoes
- Go on fabulous holiday
- Throw a party in celebration of 'single' status
- Set free the singing bird

Get a life; that'll show him, she swore
as she passed out on the kitchen floor
having somnolently opened the bird-cage door.

On waking the next morning with an almighty hangover
she phoned in sick; but her new employer
lacking a sense of humour, on the phone sacked her.

    It was not until much later
she noticed the empty cage. *Cheers*,
she raised her coffee mug to freedom –
replacing the last item on her
list with: No more lousy jobs; become a freelancer.

She then stayed in bed reviewing
    her past, present and future
until her mother came to the rescue and invited her over.

When she returned home a few days later,
she was greeted with more bird song than twitter
as she walked in through the door –

Unexpected the gift of such a treasure,
the freedom to sing with unbounded pleasure.

The Kiss

He knelt in front of her as if they were in church;
she sat there in adoration, hesitating to blemish
that gaunt face of his resembling a Russian icon
with the touch of her hands, face or lips.

They were statues carved, fingers interlocked
in prayer, perpetual communion;
they had the look of lovers that are looked upon.

Guided by love's lodestar, their ship afloat
on the high seas of life
sailing towards a destination unknown...

Through what transports of passion
breathing the same air
the distance between faces disappear
as eyes cross, embracing each other.

Prescription For Glasses

The optician adorned me with asteroid spectacles,
taking away my sight before restoring it back to me.

I was made to read the alphabets on his electric screen,
first with one eye and then the other but not with both;
letting it sink in that perfect vision was to be his gift.

We lingered in his heavily curtained, neon-lit underworld.
He sat in front of me, his scanning machine between us,
he concentrated on the state of my cornea, retina and iris.

The silence of the room was interrupted by his whispers
urging me to look at the ceiling, floor, walls on either
side, follow his phallic finger with my eyes
as it roved wildly within my arc of vision.

He bent patiently over each eye studying their defects,
his fingers pressed on my hair and temples when he turned
my head to study my profile as if he was a phrenologist.
Do you see better in this lens or in this? He queried
as he switched lenses with the dexterity of a magician.
It was difficult to say: *Is there optimal vision*?

Much depends on how much you want to see,
he muttered having explained my failure to see the world
as it is. His lenses had the gift of perfect sight –
he could mend long or short sightedness, astigmatism,
all aberrations of vision. Self-contained in a box,
unassuming, the powerful prisms of glass
stood evangelically between me and the world.

My life manageable with its ill-defined, frayed,
squinted edges. The lenses, round fish eyes,
dependable eagle eyes, alert cat eyes, beautiful in
their glassy sheen; clear as running streams in a forest.

Through the looking glass, I could see every
thing pretty much anyway I pleased.
The prescription was free.

Experience And Innocence

'Keep a thing by you
seven years
and it'll come in use
though it were the Devil,'
said Experience
when Abaddon came recently into favour.

'Unaware, I kept the Devil
seven years
locked in my heart
but learnt not its use,'
wept Innocence
when Abaddon went lately out of favour.

Daily Remedies
(For *children of all ages*)

Daily wash face with wonder,
brush teeth with honey and oil of clove;
treat itchy eyes with dewdrops and rosewater.

Swab ears regularly with raga and symphony buds;
massage body with sunshine and olive oil,
then allow to run wild in fields of grass.

Gently rub kisses into cuts and bruises;
let long hours of sleep cure aching limbs.

Treat tantrums with masterly indirection.
Listen with sympathy, slowly divert attention
towards anything that distracts them from distraction.

Answer all questions with imagination,
feed their curiosity, stretch their creativity;
with stories taller than the mightiest oaks –
reaching out for the sun, moon and stars.

Deal with stubbornness in much the same fashion,
with games, myths, songs, magic and pure illusion.

Batchelors Soup

I arrived here improvised, hesitant.
This is my life but I'm ignorant of the part.

I remain unaware of the script, unsure what the style is –
tragedy, comedy, miracle-play or puppetry?
It is poorly directed, difficult to decipher.
I make things up as I go along, being prompted
incorrectly to pull off stunts at the last minute.

I live in ignorance as I live in my skin,
there is none to question or to clarify the meaning.
I do my best under the circumstances.

I have to act without thinking, be eternally ready,
not unlike the trees outside my window, looking as if they
could do anything; put their hidden feet down, like flamingos
and take off to distant lands, green messengers of hope.

Inheriting forgiveness, the gift of forgetting, I emulate living
instinctively like any beast, bird or creeping, crawling thing.
I came here programmed with my karmic DNA.

I try not to lose the day through sorrow or apprehension,
or find myself in contemplation of what is not to be.
I empty the contents of life's sachet into this fleeting present,
add passion to taste and a perfect cup of life is ready for me.

Azaleas In Spring

It was by no means evident
that the super kinetic buzzing of bees
expressed any pleasure taken in exploring,
sucking the azaleas, full bloom in spring.

Nor did the bees behave badly, drunk with honey.

They appeared sober
gliding from bower to bower,
calm under the circumstances, robot-like,
displaying no emotion nor will power
going about their business, fertilising each flower.

Nor was it clear that the fragrant azaleas
frigid under the dervish dance of the bees
felt any ecstasy during or after
the mindless marauding of bees.

The azaleas appeared to respond eagerly
shuddering in passing gusts of wind...

Flight Distance
(With acknowledgment to Yann Martel's *Life of Pi*)

Flamingos in the wild won't mind
our presence three hundred yards off.
Cross that boundary, and they sense danger.
Get closer, and you trigger
a flight reaction from which they will
not cease until
that safe distance is re-established
or their lungs and hearts fail.

Giraffes will allow you to come near
thirty yards of them if you are
in a vehicle, but will retreat rapidly
if you come within a hundred
and fifty yards on foot.

       Fiddler crabs scurry
if you are ten yards away.
Howler monkeys stir in their branches at twenty.
African buffaloes react at seventy-five.

Cats look, deer listen, bears smell.
Male seahorses flee flashing a light of amber –

How far or near you am I allowed to venture?

Mrs Kafka's Dilemma

While he was busy
with the nature of the universe,
the incomprehensibility of God,
and other weighty matters,

She noticed a transformation in her –
when she sneezed
butterflies flew out of her nostrils,
she laughed and music emerged
accompanied by a spectacular laser show.
Weeping had much the same effect
though the sounds and colours were sombre.

Her clipped nails she sold as rice-pearls
and her tears as precious moon-stones.
All this amused her, made her popular.

The trouble began the day he metamorphosed
into a dreadful insect. The same day wherever
her hair fell, they turned into snakes.

Then a strange terror seized her –
she could finally get rid of him, perfect murder,
but could not imagine other men fancying her.

Annoyingly, part of her was in love with Franz;
though she could never be sure which part.

She covered her head with a thick black lace,
plaited her long hair tight; refused to stir
out of her room, kept her door locked;
wore herself out hiding the wretched
creatures in her washing basket
each time they mysteriously appeared
(luckily they were harmless in her hands)
before despatching them to the forest
swearing her maid to eternal secrecy.

She dreaded her husband coming to see her
fearing that sooner or later
a single strand of her own hair
would betray her, making her a liar
for confessing her snake-hair killed her partner,
that she herself was quite innocent in this matter.

Perhaps, her maid would vouch for her?
But what if no one believed her either?

If she could keep her counsel and pretend
she knew nothing about his disappearance,
could she then enlist the silence of others?

The uncertainty of it all simply destroyed her,
she knew not when these strange things
would stop happening to her.
She experienced loneliness as never before.

Nor could she predict the violence of her thoughts
if she were to witness a snake mating
with a gigantic insect before devouring it.

Broken Glass

Last night in my dream you stood in sunlight
streaming through my front door, your arms cradling
a bunch of bluebells gathered from your country home.
You had come to tell me about your wedding.

Your kingfisher blue eyes catching the light
as in a Vermeer settling on me like sea on seashells.
You had taught me what it meant to be truly desired,
each pore of my body rejoicing in our insatiable carousal.

Our loving had been more brilliant than sunsets in autumn,
setting our two landscapes on fire. It took us days
to quench our exquisite though volcanic passion.
You wanted no other man to see the face of my satisfaction.

The bluebells were fresh in your translucent vase for days
reminding me it was early spring
    in the seasons of our knowing.
How did we come to such an unseasonal end?
Why appear now like an angel with your annunciation?

With each passing breath, I died a little with you.
With each death, I learnt to live a lifetime without you.

Taking Stock

Why did he think adding meant increase?
To me it was dilution.
                Philip Larkin

I would not have bestowed my heart
if I thought you might break it in the taking.
Nor was friendship more measured in its giving.

There is no way of insuring our protection;
whether affection lives or dies is a matter of grace
which has to be earned in life like everything else.

Love need not be a puking, bawling, magical child.
There is no knowing how many ways
a mother can lose her flesh and blood.
The pain is always the same.
Life's hour-glass keeps running.

Yet women enlist in this act of creation,
not addition nor dilution
just fulfilling nature's ordination;
lending their bodies –
sometimes there is no choice
in the manner of conception –
to some purpose that transcends human recognition.

To have no partner, no child, no job or financial security
is not natural to me. I cannot say this is exactly the way
I wanted it to be. But life has a way of turning out as it does.

We are not measured by how our lives evolve for us,
only the manner of our moulding it as it is briefly lent to us.

Celebration
(For *Mimi Khalvati's* 60th birthday)

When you awake, moving into the morning,
    making do with light –
may it refract into a rainbow of bliss.

Ignore all letters and cards that remind you
of your coming of a special age!
For a letter from the Queen
you'll have to wait another 40 years;
but what about recognition for giving London
The Poetry School? *To be or not to be*
would be an interesting preoccupation –
    this your *borrowed plumage*
language, more strange than this foster-tongue
    this English, fairy godmother…

May her Majesty's Government bequeath to you
a not too meagre pension to squander on
brandy and summer gloves and satin sandals.
Pray do not grow old or practise to wear purple.
That would simply not do for you…

When you get your freedom pass
may you not be trapped in traffic jams.
Let your debts be paid off leaving you in peace;
let there be no deficit in your life's endowment
as we approach the edge of the same blackness
    trying to plumb the void's inner sense.

May your family and friends throw a secret ball
in your honour, your admirers a *Festschrift*;
may your lovers dream of your *pilgrim soul…*
(not shared *hours of pain*)
may your dreams reside in the crescent moon
growing to fullness, redeeming your wishes –
may your God hold you in the palm of his hand…
Salamat hoshid: Blessings for your new year!
May heaven and earth conspire a perfect celebration.

Fickle Flame

Swaying on tiptoe, a reluctant ballerina in discomfort,
past midnight, shivering in a bath towel in mid-winter,
leaning against a drafty bare window for support,
I yearn for the all-embracing benison of a hot shower.

The shampoo in my unwashed hair begins to trickle
into my eyes. I fumble for the ignition button of my boiler. Heady
with discovery I press passionately for the flame to rekindle,
remembering to *press repeatedly and hold until flame is steady* –

As directed in the instruction manual, now inscribed in my memory.
One finger glued to the redeeming button, I am afraid of losing
the flame that goes out, again and again. Though weary,
I woo patiently pressing incessantly, tired fingers aching.

I pirouette with joy when the boiler shudders back to life.
If only I had a button to restore belief, banish chaos and strife.

Mirrors

In the morning light shameless gleam of miniature
mirrors, so many reporters taking our semi-nude pictures;
we duck and fence not revealing our true natures.

We get minted into myriad images as we prepare
for the day in a hall of mirrors, a royal couple.

The Pipli patchwork, the Rajasthani tapestries
stuccoed with glass, beads and coin-sized eyeglasses
record all that moves within their field of vision;
not for them the transformations of the Smirnoff drinker's
imagination. Poor historians, they do what they can.

We progress through the lonely coast in a crablike manner,
never going straight for the kill but through indirection,
protecting our strategy, not declaring our intention.

Birdsong drifting through open summer windows
announces the high tide of spring, onset of summer.
Ruthless days pursue the edge of time; another afternoon
prepares to depart without us having taken a step further.

. . . *Further to what?* I hear you echo under the curved
hour-glass that holds us in, then lets us part.

Sleeping Beauty

Until we met, I did not realise
life had passed me by,
tiptoeing out of my chamber,
a guileless child retrieving its handful of toys
not wanting to disturb me in my slumber.

Then Fate cast us together and I was awakened
until you said: *All human relationships have a life-span,*

I couldn't help thinking of supermarket foods
with use-by dates embossed on each carton.
Love is done when love's begun, the sages caution.

Being weak, I keep straying into shops with 'Sale' signs on,
hunting for merchandise with lifetime guarantees.

Having mastered the art of window-shopping
as I meander through life's bazaar,
looking at shops, admiring their displays,
without asking the price of life, love and liberty –

I return to my own space, unaware of myself,
not knowing whether I am half asleep or half awake.

Patience

Four cards spread on the table, it was my turn to deal –
the Queen of Hearts blushed next to the King of Spades;
the Ace of Diamond jostled with the Knave of Clubs.
They had a lesson for me as the game was soon to reveal.

I could not have succeeded with all of you.
Hearts are fragile and tend to break. Power and wealth,
two impostors, are here today and gone tomorrow.
Knaves remain knaves, whether of Hearts or of Clubs.

I picked up one rascal from the pack to pass the time,
not knowing where our association might lead.
I was supposed to set an example like the Three Graces,
play the game of life without losing myself,
nor dictating how I wanted my life to be.

I tried again and again, hoping that fickle Luck
might have gone Cupid-blind and directed
one random arrow at me: 'It could be *you*.'

I tossed aside a lifetime of dancing, paper men
with their ramshackle house of cards,
each flawed in some unredeemable way.
I quit the game when I stumbled upon my Joker.

Earthing Live Wires

You speak of Blake, Taverner and Ginsberg
just a few of your preoccupations this week.
You share my obsession over the telephone for self-definition,
your live wire confession that aesthetics and human
affection are your vocation. I make myriad connections,
marking the boundaries of personal relations.

I will not pretend we are no different from computers
in airports that connect travellers to hotels and theatres
offering the best value for a night-out. In museums
you can be enlightened with the meaning of paintings and sculptures
with the mere pressing of a button, the insertion of a coin.

I cannot read you like a text message, nor will the direction
of my thoughts be predicted by the movement of the heavens.
Your touch electrifies me into new ways of looking at the world;
my loneliness, footloose in the galaxies of our configuration.

I will be patient and wait for us to connect each other's lives,
switching on in the fullness of time into our broadband mysteries.
We may yet get to know each another in true spirit, flesh and blood,
not in virtual reality. Anchor me in your being, your lightening rod.

Dear Tech Support

Last year I upgraded Boyfriend 5.0 to Husband 1.0
and noticed a distinct slowdown in the performance
of the flower, jewellery and other network applications
that had operated flawlessly in the Boyfriend system.

Husband 1.0 has un-installed valuable programmes,
such as Romance 9.0, Night-out 6.0, Real Passion 10.0,
and automatically installed many undesirable programmes –
Cricket 5.0, Football 8.0, and News Eternal 9.0.
The Conversation programme no longer runs as before,
and House Cleaning 4.0 simply crashes the system.

I've tried running the latest Nagging software,
adding a new welcome screen to our favourite settings;
examined all my folders, searched his documents
for evidence of infected files or commands
corrupting the Passion programme,
creative play centres and other functions.

The Husband 1.0 system has acquired a mind of its own.
It changes font colour when I paste kisses on it, where as
the Boyfriend system had positively puffed with satisfaction.
The outlook for Messenger services has deteriorated,
access to weekly live-updates no longer excel
in their power and are never to the point.

I have viewed the automatic image utility function,
zooming in on dates and times of malfunctioning,
cross-referencing every word or programme
inserted, deleted; but cannot find any rhyme or reason.

What help can you provide, dear Tech Support, in restoring
Husband 1.0 to the default configuration of Boyfriend 5.0?

Dear Customer

Be realistic and not too critical; bear in mind
that Boyfriend 5.0 was an entertainment package
but Husband 1.0 is an operating system.
A whole new concept, they cannot be compared.

Try to enter the command C: I THOUGHT YOU LOVED ME
when you switch Husband 1.0 on next, then install Tears 6.6.
Husband 1.0 should automatically run the following applications:
Guilt 7.0, Flowers 5.0, Dinner-at-your-favourite-restaurant 3.0.
But remember, overuse of this application can cause Husband 1.0
to default to Grumpy Silence 2.0 or Happy Hour 4.0.

Note that Drinking Beer 6.0 is a disruptive programme,
generating Snoring Loudly files. DO NOT install
Mother-In-Law or another Boyfriend programme.
These are not supported applications and will crash Husband 1.0.
No amount of rebooting or repair can then restore the system.

It could also trigger Husband 1.0 to default to programme
Girlfriend 10.0 that runs dormant in the background.
It has been known to introduce potentially serious viruses
into the operating system. Husband 1.0 is a great programme,
but comes with limited memory; and has been known
to be rather slow in learning new applications.

You might consider buying additional software to enhance
system performance. Personally, I recommend Hot Food 4.0,
Single-Malt Scotch 5.0 supported by Black Satin Lingerie 6.0,
which have been credited with improved hardware performance.

The Hour Glass

I lean out of your attic window,
a not-so-lithe gymnast in life's circus,
my legs balance on an unsteady ladder,
sometimes on your head and shoulder.

It was me who offered to count the missing tiles
on your roof; dealing with insurance claims
can make anyone feel lost. Floating in mid-air,
I am a pillar of strength as you mentally lean on me.
You suffer from vertigo; I have no fear of flying.

The velux window see-saws, reflects your face in
the clouds; you stand on edge, streamlined as a stalagmite,
on the spiralling staircase, steadying me with your touch.

This can't be love? I ask myself as I perch on your roof
surveying the texture of weather-beaten tiles with a field-glass.
I catch cats, birds, clouds, all independent creatures,
in my crystal cage instead of monkeys, peacocks, eagles,
and brightly coloured washing waving to the sun with
stranded paper kites stretched like bats on coconut trees.

I remember swinging in a garden on a rooftop in Bhubaneswar,
undulating with the green fields of rice; the concave blue sky,
divine hour glass, changing its features as I floated by.

Here we stand like soul-twins, houses semi-detached,
cemented in the middle by a wall of glass;
your hands connected to my feet as our glances cross over.
I climb down the ladder into the magnetic field of arms,
remove you further through the eyes of a binocular.

My Good Luck Home

You presented me with two scarabs,
hieroglyphs etched on their lapis-lazuli backs,
from the gift-shop of the British Museum.

It's for good luck, you said;
I surveyed the pieces, their sacredness
treasured in the hollow of my palm,
imagining them alive, at home in a desert.

They nestled behind a coral stone and a pearl
framed in rings of beaten gold on my fingers;
charms given by my family to protect me from evil.

I find the Egyptian scarab couple their own home
away from the crowded open-house of my Indian gods,
transforming each corner of my living room
with the gifts of fetishes from around the world.

Two Chinese cats guard my speculative angle of vision.
Even Ganesha travels with me in my handbag
to help me overcome obstacles in my adopted homeland.

The seven gods of luck from Japan smile on
as you eye my marble turtle god with its fine chiselled look,
its beady eyes, hand-crafted, appraising your secret nook –
leaving us with the legacy of an understanding –

The knowledge of what it means
to carry a whole household in oneself,
to be so perfectly self-contained, poised
at the centre of all manner of creatures unsheltered.

Loooking In, Looking Out

You remove your shoes before you climb up the stairs,
a velux window lies where the attic might have been.

A cupola of light makes all the difference to the inner
courtyard of my life. I am angle-poised, ready for vision.

It's an art gallery! You exclaim taking in the miniature
prints and paintings, works of embroidery
and windows framing landscapes richer than tapestries;
pictures changing with hours and angles of light.

The old-fashioned windows in the rest of my home
rattle like an old nanny crooning me to sleep,
stirring me to open the curtains, let the moonlight in.

You talk about new programmes in words and windows,
lost in the realm of global markets and cyber space.

Is this how I will remember your profile
against my window telling me you have decided
to spend your birthday with your parents?

I recollect opening a window in my ancestral home
to watch the electric monsoons through the night.

Tonight we open another window switching on the TV,
watch helplessly how frail windows can be
failing to protect children and women
caught in civil wars in their streets;
powerless in the face of hurricanes
rampaging through windows, doors, roofs
sweeping away homes, pillaging life and property.

I can no longer recall what it felt like to be truly desired,
I gaze into your eyes but can find no help there.

Only a memory of your voice:
Wait for things to come to you.
As we wait for things to be revealed to us,
Life and Time have their way.

Love grows wings and flies out of hearts and homes.
Love, that many-splendoured thing, will not stay
in place, be entombed and expected to rise like a saviour.

If only we could save our feelings in simple programmes,
words for windows...
       I turn to the trees outside my window.

The leaves have a session with me complaining of their fate
of having no choice, no opportunity to escape from
the light of day, rugged chefs in green,
slaves of photosynthesis;
no freedom to fly the skies like birds surveying
the earth's artistry, eyes looking out, looking in...

The mind's windows are uniquely tainted. My thoughts
dance feverishly on the stained-glass windows of my cathedral
swooning like flies against walls that limit my explorations.